Weekend CAMPING
COOKBOOK

Over 100
**Delicious Recipes for
Campfire and Grilling**

FOX CHAPEL
PUBLISHING

© 2022 by Fox Chapel Publishing Company, Inc., 903 Square Street, Mount Joy, PA 17552.

Recipe selection, design, and book design © Fox Chapel Publishing.
Recipes and photographs © G&R Publishing DBA CQ Products.

ISBN 978-1-4971-0293-4

Library of Congress Control Number: 2021945325

The following images are credited to Shutterstock.com and their respective creators: page 8: AlexMaster; page 11: Pasko Maksim; page 12: VDB Photos; page 13: James Steidle; page 25: Iris photo; page 26: GSDesign; page 37: Carol Provins; page 53: Geartooth Productions; page 54: LittleMiss; page 60: Hong Vo; page 69: Harlan Schwartz; page 83: EvdokiMari; page 91: Samuel Scranton; page 105: LaurieSH; pages throughout, texture: Art ink studio; cover, main: Kevin Capretti; cover, first row left: Serhii Opikanets; cover, first row middle: Josie Grant; cover, first row right: encierro; cover, second row left: Melissa Balthaser; cover, second row middle: Serhii Opikanets; cover, third row right: ShaduraViktor; folio icon throughout: cgterminal.

To learn more about the other great books from Fox Chapel Publishing, or to find a retailer near you, call toll-free 800-457-9112 or visit us at *www.FoxChapelPublishing.com*.

We are always looking for talented authors. To submit an idea, please send a brief inquiry to acquisitions@foxchapelpublishing.com.

Printed in China
Third printing

33

59

107

CONTENTS

8 Introduction

13 Chapter 1: Breakfast

25 Chapter 2: Hamburgers, Hot Dogs, and One-Dish Mains

37 Chapter 3: Grilled Sandwiches

53 Chapter 4: Sinful Sides and Comfort Carbs

69 Chapter 5: Veggies

83 Chapter 6: Fruit

91 Chapter 7: Desserts and S'mores

105 Chapter 8: Snacks and Appetizers

112 Index

RECIPES

13 Chapter 1: Breakfast

14   Carrot Cake Pancakes
15   Cowboy Camp Coffee
15   Iced Coffee
16   Flaky Walnut Pastries
17   Cheesy Bacon Buns
18   Bacon and Potato Pancakes
19   Fluffy Flapjacks
20   Berry-licious French Toast
21   Overnight Apple Pie Oatmeal
22   Almond French Toast
22   Honey Bran Muffins
23   Strawberry Frenchies
24   Breakfast Tarts
24   Bacon Quiche Tarts

25 Chapter 2: Hamburgers, Hot Dogs, and One-Dish Mains

26   Skillet Kielbasa Hash
28   Hawaiian Roasts
28   Hobo Burgers
29   Sweet Potato Black Bean Chili
30   Bow Wow Hot Dogs
30   Hot Dawgs
31   Garden Pup Hot Dogs
31   Canine Kraut Hot Dogs
32   Southwestern Chicken and Rice Dinner
32   All-American Burger
33   Chicken Enchilada Skillet
34   Stuffed Frankfurters
34   Favorite Cheddar Burger
35   Sausage Pizza on a Stick
36   Blue Cheese and Bacon Stuffed Burgers
36   Meatloaf Burgers

38

51

37 Chapter 3: Grilled Sandwiches

38   Apple-Cinnamon Grilled Cheese

39   Inside-Out Jalapeño Poppers

40   Cheesy Spinach Calzones

42   Sloppy Joes

43   Toasted BLT

44   Peanut Butter Waffles

45   Stuffed Toast

46   Hot Chicken Salad Pitas

47   S'mores Hand Pies

48   Reubens on the Fire

48   Grilled Cheese Perfection

49   Philly Cheesesteaks

50   Quick Quesadillas

51   Avocado Tuna Melts

52   Hot Sourdough Deli Sandwiches

53 Chapter 4: Sinful Sides and Comfort Carbs

54   Baby Reds

56   Grilled Potato Salad

57   Potato Salad Onions

58   Alfredo Mac and Cheese

59   Dutch Oven Cornbread

60   Three-Cheese Mac with Brussels Sprouts

62   Cheesy Jalapeño Loaf

63   Quick Sweet Potatoes and Apples

63   Basic Grilled Potato Packets

63   BBQ Baked Beans

64   Herbed New Potatoes

64   Bacon Corn Muffins

65   Brie Bread

66   Bacon-Wrapped Onions

66   Basic Potatoes in Foil

67   Stuffed Cheese Bread

68   Grill-Baked Sweet Potatoes

56

57

68

78

81

85

69 Chapter 5: Veggies

70 Garlic and Onion Asparagus
71 Cauliflower with Parmesan
72 Broccoli Casserole
72 Citrus Broccoli and Carrots
73 Simply Carrots
74 Rainbow Pinwheels
75 Artichokes and Carrots
75 Asian Asparagus
76 Cauliflower with Spicy Cheese Sauce
76 Mozzarella and Tomato Skewers
77 Italian Snap Peas
78 Layered Veggie Salad
79 Foiled Cabbage
80 Veggie Pizza
80 Layered Lettuce
81 Picnic Foil Pack
82 Campfire Green Beans

83 Chapter 6: Fruit

84 Piña Colada Pineapple Sticks
85 Firecracker Watermelon
86 Peachy Mallow
86 Roasted Peaches
86 Grilled Bananas
87 Fruit Puffs
88 Fruity Bread Pudding
88 Foiled Peaches
89 Bacon-Wrapped Cantaloupe
90 Pears in Caramel Sauce
90 Fruit Pizza

74

89

91 Chapter 7: Desserts and S'mores

92 S'more Burritos
92 Gingerbread Cake in an Orange Shell
93 Zesty Orange S'mores
93 Strawberry Cream S'mores
94 Lemon Coconut S'mores
94 Choco Raspberry S'mores
95 Grilled Cherry Chocolate Pizza
96 Campfire Cones
97 Cashew Brownie S'mores
97 Bacon S'mores
98 Apple Pie S'mores
98 Strawberry Nutella Banana S'mores
99 Tropical S'mores
99 Sailor S'mores
100 Fudgy Orange Campfire Cakes
101 Strawberry Shortcakes
102 Toasted Coconut Pumpkin Pies
103 Lemon-Lemon S'mores
103 Party Pastry S'mores
104 Cinnamon Sensation S'mores
104 Minty Mix S'mores

105 Chapter 8: Snacks and Appetizers

106 Grape Thyme Appetizers
106 Munch Munch
107 Chocolate Peanut Butter Hummus
107 Roasted Nuts
108 Corn and Black Bean Guacamole
108 Phyllo Bites
109 Cast Iron Nachos
110 Stuffed Baby Peppers
110 Fire-Roasted Pickle Wraps
111 Popcorn Packs
111 Mushroom and Bacon Bites

INTRODUCTION

Camping suggests tranquil simplicity. Communing with nature. Effortless relaxation. Sunlight sparkling on water. Drifting off to sleep with the scent of clean dirt and pine on a gentle breeze. Weekend camping is a great escape from the everyday experience.

Still, you have to eat and that's ok! Food adds tremendously to the camping getaway. It tastes better when you're camping. And it's easier because you can do the planning, shopping, prep, and even the cooking before you go. Anything that can be done ahead of time and tossed on the campfire is weekend camping food at its finest.

Weekend Camping Cookbook is premised upon that fundamental idea. More than 100 recipes are included in these pages that you can prep, make, freeze or chill, pack, and eat. Stress-free,

delicious, fun, and filling foods for every meal and appetite, guaranteed.

Enjoy choosing your favorites, and when it comes time to eat on the weekend, use the following handy helpful tips to keep your campfire cooking easy.

DESTRESSING YOUR TRIP
Remember to read through your chosen recipes before you go and plan ahead for ways you can make your life easier at camp.
- Pre-mix your dry ingredients, fillings, and spices and store them in labeled zippered plastic bags or air-tight containers.
- Note which recipes have make-at-home options and prepare and pack those ahead of time.

CAMP COOKING TOOLS YOU MIGHT NEED

- ☐ paper goods (paper towels, napkins)
- ☐ dish cloths and towels
- ☐ tableware— silverware, plates, bowls, and cups
- ☐ a first-aid kit
- ☐ leather gloves/oven mitts/potholders
- ☐ a spatula
- ☐ stirring and slotted spoons
- ☐ a whisk
- ☐ sharp knives

- ☐ a long, metal spatula
- ☐ long, metal tongs
- ☐ a long, metal meat fork
- ☐ measuring cups and spoons
- ☐ a can opener
- ☐ a bottle opener
- ☐ a pair of scissors
- ☐ a long lighter and matches
- ☐ a digital meat thermometer

- ☐ propane or charcoal
- ☐ dry wood, kindling wood, newspaper, and fire starters
- ☐ heavy-duty foil and foil pans
- ☐ a baking sheet
- ☐ a cast iron pan
- ☐ a muffin tin
- ☐ a Dutch oven
- ☐ skewers
- ☐ a pie iron
- ☐ an over-the-fire grate

- Buy shredded or sliced vegetables and cheese so you don't have to do that prep work yourself.
- Create a list of additional food items you might need for camp, such as hamburger or hot dog rolls, additional spices, or nonstick cooking spray.
- Finally, review the **Camp Cooking Tools You Might Need checklist** to be sure you've packed all the cooking and safety items you might need.

Above all, stay flexible and have fun. If you forget something, you can improvise without worry! Skillet meals can easily be turned into foil pack or pie iron meals and seasonings and toppings can be adjusted based on what you have available. Your campfire meals can be as much of an adventure as the trip itself!

CAMPFIRE SAFETY TIPS AND TRICKS

- Make sure it is legal to build a fire in your location.
- Use a fire pit, if available. Otherwise, build your fire on rock or dirt and construct a U-shaped perimeter with large rocks.
- Build your fire at least 8' away from flammable objects.
- Never use gas or kerosene on a fire as they pose a serious risk of explosion.
- Never leave a fire unattended.
- Don't build a fire if it's windy. Sparks can cause unintended fires.
- Protect hands with leather gloves or heavy oven mitts and use long tongs to prevent burns.
- Fill a bucket with water and keep it near the fire to douse flare-ups.
- Extinguish your fire by dousing it with plenty of water. Be sure all the coals, embers, and wood are wet and cool.
- If you don't have access to water, smother the fire with sand or dirt to extinguish it. You should still be sure all the coals, embers, and wood are completely cool.

BUILDING THE PERFECT COOKING FIRE

First things first: you'll only get a nice cooking fire if you use the right kind of firewood. Use split logs since they produce the best heat and are easiest to ignite. Hard woods such as maple, walnut, oak, or apple are best; they burn slowly and produce wonderful cooking coals.

Pile up tinder in the cooking area; light with a match or lighter. When the tinder is burning well, place kindling loosely on top, adding more as needed. Once the kindling is burning nicely, carefully add split firewood, teepee-style, over the burning kindling.

When the flames die down, white hot coals remain. Use a metal fire poker or long stick to distribute the coals for cooking, as needed.

CAMPFIRE COOKING BASICS

Whatever method of cooking you choose—grill, foil, pie iron, skewer—remember to grease it before cooking. If camping with kids, adult supervision is essential! Only a few people can safely cook around a campfire at once, so campers should take turns, be nice, and avoid poking or chasing anyone with sharpened sticks or flaming marshmallows.

Foil Cooking

Heavy-duty foil is a camper's best friend. It has multiple uses and makes for easy clean-up. Foil packs work best on a two-inch bed of coals and will heat up quickly. You can use a few different types of foil packs. Remember that it is better to use too much foil than too little. Watch for steam and use potholders or oven mitts and long tongs to handle foil packs. Place them on baking sheets to move to and from your campfire.

Food wrapped in airtight foil packs will be steamed, not toasted or crunchy. For crisp foods, make and bake food in open foil pans. Make an open baking pan by using a double layer of heavy-duty foil molded over an upside-down pan of your choice. Leave extra length at all edges, fold them over, and crimp well for strength. You can also make a griddle for sautéing or frying foods over a campfire by covering a wire rack, grate, or grill with a double layer of heavy-duty foil.

Skewer Cooking

Skewers are useful for easily cooking kebabs and other camp-friendly dishes. If you are using wooden skewers, soak them in water for 30 minutes to reduce the risk of creating little flaming sticks. If using metal skewers with wooden handles, keep the handles away from direct heat, too.

Pie Iron Cooking

Pie irons are amazingly versatile. The hinged cooker allows you to cook nearly any ingredients into a satisfying pie-shaped meal—grilled sandwiches, scrambled eggs, and even pies cook quick and easy. Some pie irons can also be separated into two halves, which you can use like mini skillets.

FOIL PACK TECHNIQUES

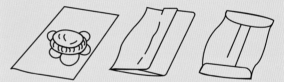

FLAT PACKS work best for cooking meat, fish, and foods that need less steam and more browning.

TENT PACKS are best for cooking vegetables, fruits, and combination packs that need more steam and less browning.

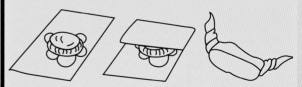

TWO-HANDLED PACKS are useful if you want to bury your foil packs in coals. Use tongs to grab the handles and pull the packs out of the coals.

CAMPFIRE COOKING TEMPERATURES

How long can you hold your hand 4" over the coals?

- 2 seconds = about 500°F (High heat)
- 3 seconds = about 400°F (Medium-High heat)
- 4 seconds = about 350°F (Medium heat)
- 5 seconds = about 300°F (Low heat)

COOKING TIMES WILL VARY

Since speed of cooking depends on the temperature of the campfire and the type of food being cooked, use the cooking times suggested in each recipe as approximates, but check cooking progress often (carefully). Thick foods and frozen or refrigerated foods will take longer to cook than thinner foods or foods starting at room temperature.

You can adjust the temperature of your embers or coals by moving them apart and you can adjust the heat getting to your food by placing the food beside the coals on rocks or on a grill or grate above the coals. Turning your food often will also help evenly distribute the heat.

A Note on Campfire Cooking Temperatures

Some of the recipes recommend cooking over a fire that is a certain heat level or temperature. You can use the following method to judge the temperature of your campfire. Hold your hand about 4" over the coals. Count the number of seconds you can hold your hand in place before it gets too hot to keep it there.

- 2 seconds = about 500°F (High heat)
- 3 seconds = about 400°F (Medium-High heat)
- 4 seconds = about 350°F (Medium heat)
- 5 seconds = about 300°F (Low heat)

Food Temperature Safety

No matter the heat of your fire, always make sure your food is thoroughly cooked. Ground meat, chicken, and pork should be cooked until it is no longer pink and juices run clear. But color isn't a fool-proof guide. It is best to use a good meat thermometer to prevent under- or over-cooking. The USDA recommends the following minimum internal temperatures:

- Fish: 145°F
- Beef Roasts: 145°F (rare) to 160°F (medium) to 170°F (well-done)
- Ground Beef: 160°F
- Ground Poultry: 165°F
- Chicken Breasts: 170°F

- Whole Poultry and Parts (thighs, wings): 180°F
- Pork (chops, tenderloins): 160°F
- Ground Pork: 160°F
- Egg Dishes: 160°F
- Reheating Foods: 165°F or until hot and steaming

REMEMBER! Your weekend adventure will be a relaxing escape from the everyday. You've done all the work already, now it's time to hit the road. Double check your recipes and lists to make sure you have everything you need, then pack up your tent and sleeping bags for a fun weekend escape.